MAGNIFICENT PLACES

Oregon Coast

Photography by Rick Schafer

Essays by Jack and Jan McGowan

GRAPHIC ARTS CENTER PUBLISHING®

*To all those who help to preserve and protect
our wonderful Oregon Coast.*

Rick Schafer and Jack and Jan McGowan

International Standard Book Number 1-55868-1-55868-250-3
Library of Congress Number 96-75308
Photographs © MCMXCVI by Rick Schafer
Essays © MCMXCVI by Graphic Arts Center Publishing Company
No part of this book may be copied by any means
without written permission from the publisher.
President • Charles M. Hopkins
Editor-in-Chief • Douglas A. Pfeiffer
Managing Editor • Jean Andrews
Photo Editor • Diana S. Eilers
Designer • Robert Reynolds
Production Manager • Richard L. Owsiany
Book Manufacturing • Lincoln & Allen Co.
Printed and Bound in the United States of America

Page i: At the top of the food chain in their ecosystem, starfish grace tidal pools and help maintain environmental balance. *Page ii:* Sand, shells, and gravel bear the punishment of relentless waves. *Page iii:* The Cape Blanco lighthouse began service in 1875 to protect ships at sea. *Pages iv-v:* Haystack Rock, the third-highest coastal monolith in the world at 235 feet, rises above the surf just offshore from Cannon Beach. *Frontispiece:* Beachcombers are dwarfed by spindrift-topped waves. *Opposite Page:* Roosevelt elk, like this one at Jewell, wander the Coast Range. The largest land mammal of the northwest coast, bulls range from six to nine hundred pounds.

INTRODUCTION. Oregonians love their coast, taking her on her own terms. Rare are the bikini-hot days that draw visitors to beaches in other places. Rather, pouring rain, fog, creeping mists, and cold wind are familiar to all who spend time on Oregon's beaches. We value these moods, reveling in a storm's power, lifting our faces to a soft mist, bundling up to go outside, and seeking shelter from which to view the pounding surf. These times only help us better appreciate the sun when it does appear.

There is a healing quality in being on a beach or a headland overlooking the ocean. A cool wind coming ashore after uninterrupted miles at sea has a cleansing power that carries away stress and sorrow. Winds also carry mists that nurture coastal flora, so inland species flourish unbelievably. Salal grows knee high east of the Coast Range; here it towers overhead in dense thickets. The fauna, too, is rich and diverse—from whales to sand crabs, elk to tufted puffins.

◁ In 1788, early explorer Robert Gray, aboard the *Lady Washington*, was the first white man to see the Columbia River. Built in 1929, the Astoria Column in Astoria depicts the history of the area. ▷▷ Low tide exposes fragile tidal pools around The Needles at Cannon Beach, named for the cannon that washed ashore from the USN *Shark*, which was wrecked near here in 1846.

Large Native American settlements thrived in this environment, because of the lush resources. They felled the great trees to make canoes and build houses. They hunted and fished and gathered local produce.

The abundance of natural resources also brought European settlers to Oregon's coast. Trappers and fur traders arrived first, followed by pioneers, who built towns around logging and fishing. Today, some towns have incorporated farming commodities such as cranberries and dairy cattle as sustaining industries; many cater to visitors with hotels, shops, and restaurants.

THE NORTH COAST

Oregon's 362-mile coastline begins in the north at the Columbia River, the largest waterway in the western United States. Its statistics are awesome; its estuary, more than five miles wide. Its average discharge is 262 thousand cubic feet of water per second—thirty thousand train cars of water hurling into the Pacific each minute. Its bar, where this rushing water meets the ocean, is notorious for danger lurking beneath the surface. Some two thousand boats and ships have been wrecked since the 1800s.

The fur trade built Astoria, the city at the Columbia's mouth. Its port draws ships from around the world, loaded with agricultural products and automobiles, fuel and fish. Ships arrive daily from Asia and South America heading for inland ports such as Longview and Portland. Cargoes go from there by truck and train far into the interior of the country. Originally established by John Jacob Astor in 1811 as a fur trading center, Astoria is the oldest settlement west of the Mississippi continuously occupied by Europeans.

For a visual history, visit the Astoria Column on Coxcomb Hill. Murals on this lighthouse-like structure depict scenes from Native American life, western exploration, and pioneer settlement. Inside, a 166-step spiral staircase leads to an observation deck. The view is definitely worth the climb, especially at sunset when Oregon's often cloudy skies create a perfect canvas for the pinks, purples, and oranges of day's end. A wind is likely blowing—the Oregon Coast wind that leaves you feeling clear-headed and slightly out of breath.

◁ Haystack Rock, rising 235 feet above the ocean floor at Cannon Beach, is possibly the best-known icon of the Oregon Coast. Here, it is mirrored with such phenomenal clarity one finds it difficult to differentiate between sky and water. Monoliths of this type, common all along the Oregon Coast, become more predominent farther south. Their varied forms often inspire poetic names.

Meriwether Lewis and William Clark made their camp near today's Fort Stevens, just south of Astoria, in the winter of 1805-06. They had traveled more than four thousand miles, from the mouth of the Missouri River, on the first official exploration to the west by the US government. The camp was vital to a successful return trip. Low on supplies, in ill health and wearing rotting clothes, the explorers made good use of local resources. They extracted salt from sea water, killed 131 elk and 20 deer, and made new clothes from animal skins. They built cabins and furniture, collected fuel, prepared food, and regained their strength. Fort Astoria, a replica of the camp, is interesting as a historical snapshot. Botanical markers around the park identify native plants and begin to give you a sense of the abundance of edible and useful materials available in the wild.

Geologists say the land from Astoria south to Tillamook was formed some twenty million years ago, when today's Coast Range was still under water. Basalt lava flows underlie the higher hills. Offshore, the erosion of overlying mudstones created the uniquely beautiful seastack formations, more abundant the farther south you travel. Haystack Rock at Cannon Beach is the largest monolith of this type in the world.

South from Astoria are Seaside and Cannon Beach, as different as two towns in such close proximity can be. Seaside boasts a decorative sea wall complete with promenade and lamp posts, circa 1920, along two miles of its flat, sandy beach. "The prom" is a

▷ A collection of lanterns at the Columbia River Maritime Museum in Astoria tells a tale of the thousands of items from ships of many types that have penetrated inland from the sea. The museum houses maritime memorabilia from ship models to entire boats. Historical displays take you to the days of steamboat traffic on the Columbia or the bridge of a World War II destroyer.

BEACONS
&
BUOY LIGHTS

delightful place for an evening stroll or perfect for an afternoon bike ride. About midway is the turnaround, where the street circles a statue commemorating the Lewis and Clark exploration. A contingent of the encamped expedition came here to extract salt from the sea water.

Turn inland from the prom, and downtown Seaside is, well, Seaside. It is a sideshow of amusement that youngsters throughout the state know and love as the destination for family vacations—especially spring break.

Cannon Beach is a popular artist's community, with restaurants, shops, and galleries lining its charming main street. Wide sidewalks invite browsing. Benches in the main downtown courtyard provide a break from shopping. A beautiful broad beach edges the town, and Ecola State Park anchors it on the north. The park abounds with wildlife, including deer and numerous birds, and affords beautiful walking trails. The close proximity of natural beauty and urban center help explain Cannon Beach's popularity.

South of Cannon Beach is a long stretch of natural areas, including seven state parks and waysides that provide parking and pathways to the beach. A few small towns, such as Manzanita, Nehalem, and Rockaway, offer quiet escapes for visitors. The Nehalem River meets the ocean here. Rain and mist rising from the Pacific catch in the Coast Range mountains on their inland journey. The droplets find their way along fir needles and broad leaves, gathering to fall in rivulets to the ground. The water flows

◁ A replica of the encampment of Lewis and Clark's Expedition brings the winter of the 1805-1806 expedition to life. Meriwether Lewis and William Clark were commissioned by President Jefferson to lead the first American foray through what is now the western United States. Their winter days at Fort Clatsop were spent in preparation for their arduous return trip back home.

together to form small creeks and streams, tumbling over rocks, swelling, rushing back to the sea. The drainage from more than one hundred miles of Coast Range fills the Nehalem River. Ending their journey in its broad estuary, the waters become quiet; drifting in a boat through marsh-like growth provides an unforgettable feeling of solitude. When the tall reeds obscure the shoreline, it feels as if you have traveled back in time, becoming the only person within a hundred miles. Fishing and crabbing are legend in the estuary.

Another legend surrounds Neahkahnie Mountain, the imposing headland just to the north. Native Americans told early pioneers that a great ship ran aground here, and that a large chest was carried onto the headland. Historians believe the ship may have been the Spanish galleon *San Augustin,* lost on November 30, 1595, en route from Manila to Acapulco. Beeswax, a major cargo of that time, is said to still wash up on local beaches. Hundreds have searched for the lost chest, but the mountain still holds its secret.

Tillamook Bay is the end of the journey for the Tillamook, Trask, Wilson, Kilchis and Miami Rivers. They come together in a complex tapestry of history. The Tillamook Pioneer Museum is a gem, documenting not only the immigration of the pioneers, but the rich life of Native Americans in the area. Some of that beeswax from Neahkahnie Mountain can even be seen here.

▷ The setting sun bronzes sky and water, challenging the beauty of even the most tropical locales. The sea, which seems to be so powerful, is at the same time extremely fragile. Its ecosystems have been disturbed by the hand of man over the centuries—but today many caring individuals are turning their attention to protecting and restoring this mysterious natural resource.

Loggers and mountain men helped shape local history, as did the military by building the world's largest all-wood structures here, in 1943, to house blimps. One hangar is still visible as you drive south from Tillamook.

Farther inland, three successive fires—known collectively as the Tillamook Burn—decimated 270 thousand acres of old growth forest in the Coast Range in 1933. Succored by the soft mists that normally drift in from the ocean, the firs had grown to enormous height and width. In photos of the time, loggers stand next to downed trunks much larger in diameter than the loggers are tall. In the dry heat of August, those giant firs fueled fires that devastated timber then valued at $275 million. I remember my grandmother speaking of the smoky smell and skies darkened by ash at their farm seventy miles inland. In Tillamook, two feet of ash fell, and smoke from the fires could be seen five hundred miles out at sea.

◁ A breeze off the water stirs the American flag over this tribute to Lewis and Clark in downtown Seaside. It commemorates the point visited by members of the expedition to establish saltworks. Five men traveled the five miles from Fort Clatsop, Lewis and Clark's winter camp. They rendered fourteen hundred gallons of seawater into three and one-half bushels of salt.

A thin peninsula nearly encloses Tillamook Bay, giving the towns on its eastern shore a bit of distance and protection from the pounding ocean. Garibaldi may be best known for its fishing fleets, but the big G that sits on the hill above town is a landmark dear to many. As children on family outings, we held contests to see who could pay attention well enough to be the first to see it.

Oceanside is a delightful town that sits on the peninsula, right on the ocean. A state wayside provides access to a beach protected on the north by a basalt cliff that tumbles into the ocean, splitting into a number of sea stacks. They are perfectly aligned to provide a dramatic foil for the late spring setting sun. The cool wind makes your senses come alive as the slivers of red slide past the jutting rocks and into the dark ocean beyond.

South from Tillamook, State 101 turns inland and skirts wildlife refuges and a national forest. A more scenic road hugs the coastline, revealing beach after beach and climbing to high lookout points above the ocean. Among the awe-inspiring views are the dunes and cliffs at Cape Kiwanda. Basalt sea stacks guard the fifty-million-year-old sand and mud stones, allowing the winds and water to erode them only partially. The cliffs have taken on beautiful shapes; their colors glow when touched by the sun.

If this were not sufficient, some of the most interesting and accessible tidal pools on the northern coast are found here. As ocean waters recede, they reveal rocks containing small pools teeming with sea life. A surge of wave draws the tentacles of pale green sea anemones with it. They wave gently. Tiny fish flash by, and crabs scurry from rock to rock. Sea stars enchant with their shapes and colors. It is a delicate, watery world.

While the ecosystem of the pools has evolved to need the conditions provided by receding tides, people are a relatively new part of the equation, especially the numbers that now visit the tide pools. Too many people do not leave the pools' exotic creatures as they find them, and some species are declining alarmingly.

▷ From Ecola State Park, clouds tower above the Tillamook Head lighthouse, which was completed in 1881. The lighthouse, widely known as "Terrible Tilly," was in service until 1957. It is now a columbarium—a repository for the ashes of the deceased. Today, Tillamook Rock lies more than a mile offshore from Tillamook Head, but it was once part of the mainland.

◁ Flora, such as this tree at Cannon Beach, is shaped by winds that dry and kill buds on the windward side before they open. △ At Hug Point State Park, the sculpted sands and waterfall evoke a formal Japanese Garden. ▷ ▷ Five rivers drain the Coast Range into Tillamook Bay.

△ For centuries, Native Americans have fished for numerous species while enjoying the beauty of the sea. Today, many Oregonians, Native and non-Native alike, fish in the sea itself and in the rivers, estuaries, and streams. Regulations now help to manage the resource.

△ Nautical blue and white at the Cape Meares lighthouse recalls the age of navigation by beacons. The nine lighthouses that line Oregon's coastline were all built between 1857 and the end of the century. Since that time, several have had to be replaced, the last one in 1934.

△ Guarded by basalt seastacks, the sandstones of Cape Kiwanda have been merely weathered by the waves; gorgeous colors remain today while they have been completely worn away in other coastal locations.

△ The Heceta Head lighthouse, situated just north of the famous Sea Lion Caves, was completed in 1894 at a cost of $180,000. The first order lens, contrary to those used in most American lighthouses, was not Parisian but English, manufactured by the Chance Brothers.

△ Salishan Lodge was designed to take full advantage of its beautiful setting, blending its structures and golf courses into native surroundings. ▷ Thirty-two thousand dunes move seasonally with the winds at Oregon Dunes National Recreation Area.

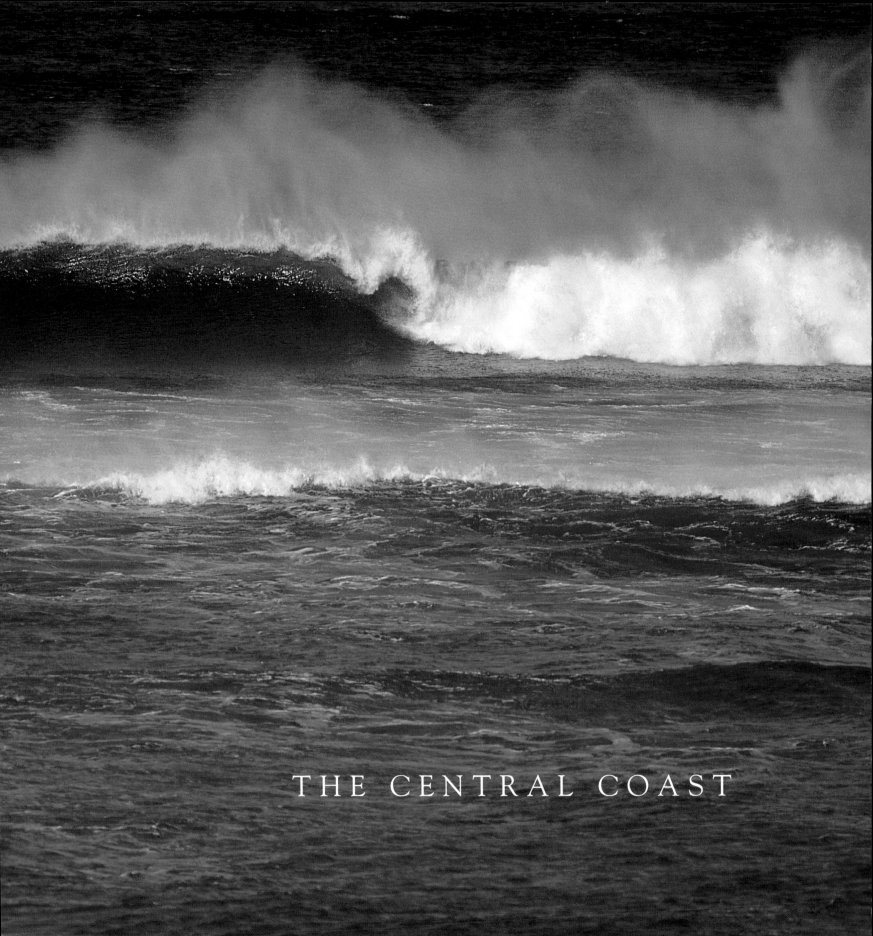

THE CENTRAL COAST

Highway 101 meanders back to the ocean at the small town of Neskowin, only to be forced inland again by the massive bulk of Cascade Head. Looking up at this soaring land mass jutting into the sky, it is sometimes possible to see weather different from that at sea level. On a sunny day below the steep south side, you may be surprised to tilt your head back and find the top obscured by clouds, with bands of rain shading its fields. From sea level, the trees and grasses on this beautiful nature center form a mosaic of stunning earth tones, the colors changing with the seasons.

A hike up the steep headland trail reveals a bounty of natural life. Birds are plentiful, as are deer and elk, which regularly wander into nearby developments. The plant life changes with the rising elevation, and the woodland smells mingle with the salt air in an intoxicating mixture.

◁ Spindrift is left behind as pounding surf meets offshore winds. Access to Oregon's central coast was difficult over the Coast Range, so it was among the last places in Oregon settled by Westerners. When entrepreneurs did arrive, they promoted fresh air and water at health spas, luring visitors from inland. The visitor industry still thrives, with grand views and excellent facilities.

At low tide, the Salmon River joins the ocean on the south side of Cascade Head with a final rush against the head's inaccessible wall of black rock. The incoming tide fills the river mouth with sea water and calms the rushing waters.

Just across the river, at the end of a tiny peninsula, is a classic sand beach that is reachable only by crossing the water. At slack tide, deer swim across. Most people prefer to bring a boat and row, perhaps throwing a crab pot overboard en route to be retrieved on the return trip.

Headlands and swales are typical of the environment along the Oregon Coast, as are certain kinds of beaches. Some of the beaches, like Cape Lookout on the northern Oregon coast, are covered with rocks and shells. Most are sand, packed firm by the surf below the high tide mark, loose and deep above. That loose sand is just meant to be walked in barefoot. It traps the sun's warmth in the top layer so that on a hot day your skin can barely stand the heat. Then, when you can't stand to take another step, you can stop and sink your feet deep into the sand. The texture caresses you; the coolness is blissful. On a cooler day the top warmth is to be reveled in.

The salt marshes of the Salmon River give way to Lincoln City on the south, a long narrow urban strip that blends what was originally five small towns. Lincoln City's shops, malls, restaurants, and hotels make up the longest continuously developed area along the Oregon Coast.

Even in this sometimes congested corridor, you are never more than a few minutes from a public access point, and the air always has a tangy salt smell. Step onto a sandy beach a short distance from the crowds, face seaward, and the fresh westerly wind carries the sounds of the city inland, leaving only the continuous roar of the waves. Close your eyes, and you are alone on a beach. Breathe in the sea smells, and you can feel the tension drop away.

Some of the first Western settlers on the central coast were entrepreneurs who built spas, which they promoted as advantageous to the health and constitutions of valley dwellers. Oregon's first resort hotel, the

▷ Nestled in quiet hideaways, coastal cottages offer a chance for many Oregonians to spend time away from hectic city workdays. Activities such as gardening, reading, or decorating can be pursued with the constant, soothing sounds of the ocean as background music. Many people also make handicrafts, creating a variety of artistic objects from driftwood and beach grass.

Ocean House, was built in 1865 in Newport, the first central Oregon coast town to be developed. Newport blossomed in the late 1800s as the destination of "summer people" from Corvallis and Portland. They arrived first by stage and later by trains. Families moved for the season; husbands commuted for weekends.

Newport's Old Town hugs the bay that is formed by the Yaquina River, and a large fishing fleet docks at the marina. Their catch is salmon, bottom fish, and shellfish destined for the canneries. The marine air mixes with the smell of the catch in a pungent concoction that is instantly recognizable as the waterfront in Newport. Fresh seafood is *de rigueur* in Newport's restaurants. The catch also draws the sea lions that lounge on the docks and play in the bay.

◁ Well-kept Coast Guard stations dot the Oregon coastline. This one in Newport offers a stunning view of the Yaquina Bay Bridge. The Coast Guard enforces customs, guards against smuggling, and is in charge of marine inspection, navigation, and lifesaving duties. In peacetime, the Coast Guard is under the Department of Transportation, but is part of the Navy during war.

Two excellent scientific research facilities in Newport are open to visitors. Both have displays that help explain the fragile ecosystems of the Oregon Coast. The first, the Hatfield Marine Science Center, has a research staff from Oregon State University and numerous excellent exhibits about the marine environment and stewardship. The aquarium, which features an octopus that can be petted, is one of the highlights of a visit here.

At the Oregon Coast Aquarium, replicas of tidal pools, churning water spouts, and an aviary bring some of the diversity of the Oregon Coast up close. The marine displays—especially Oregon's famous new resident, Keiko, who starred in the movie, "Free Willy"—help visitors understand the coastal wildlife, botany, and ecosystems and the damage that can be caused by not using care on the Coast. The replica tidal pool, which encourages careful hands-on experience, is a better place to handle the native species than the natural pools that so intrigue us. Guides oversee what is picked up, and how, and can identify the different animals.

State parks punctuate the central Oregon coast, providing beach access, picnicking, camping and spectacular views. The diversity of geologic formations makes the drive south truly a magical experience.

Driving southward, watch for spouting horns. These rare marine displays are created when incoming waves are funneled into long rock channels, where they gather speed before bursting against the rocky walls and shooting into the air in a sparkling froth of water and foam.

Sometimes the wind pushes the spouting water into lovely fan-like shapes; sometimes the mist is carried ashore to soak unwary visitors. Some of the best places to see spouting horns are at Boiler Bay State Wayside and at Depoe Bay between Lincoln City and Newport. Look north from the parking lot at Boiler Bay, or stop at the visitor center in Depoe Bay.

The *Darlingtonia californica* or pitcher plant, a rare carnivorous plant, can be seen at the Darlingtonia Botanical Wayside north of Florence. The town of Florence is situated at the mouth of the Siuslaw River,

▷ A spouting horn can be easily viewed at Depoe Bay. Depoe Bay was named for a Native American, Charlie Depoe, who got his name from living at an army depot. He later changed the spelling to Depot, but the town is still Depoe. Another spouting horn is at Boiler Bay, named for the boiler, still visible at low tide, of the steam schooner *J. Marhoffer* that sank here in 1910.

Native American for "Faraway Waters." The river was an early route into the forests of the Coast Range.

Children and adults alike delight in hunting for agates on Oregon's beaches. Plentiful in many areas such as Agate Beach, north of Newport, the beautiful translucent stones appear like rare gems at the tide line, or cover a beach as if a treasure chest had been upended there. Agates come from mineral deposits left in holes in volcanic rocks and freed when the surrounding rock erodes. They can be icy white, pale yellow, golden, orange—or shot through with a variety of colors. Wave action and sand polish the pebbles to a glossy sheen, and few are the visitors to an agate-studded beach who can resist picking up a pocketful.

Whale watching is the highlight of many spring and fall visits to Oregon's beaches. When the whales are migrating, visitors flock to the coast for a glimpse. Gray whales are the most common, although Humpback, Killer, and Sperm Whales can also be seen. All migrate south from October through December, returning north between March and May. Their twelve-thousand-mile round trip from the Bering Sea to Baja California is the longest migration undertaken by any mammal in the world.

Any point that juts out into the ocean is good for whale watching, especially if it is elevated a little. You may find yourself imagining a spray as a whale. Could it be, or is it just two waves coming together at sea?

◁ The Yaquina Head Lighthouse, built in 1873, was intended to be constructed at Otter Crest to the north. The materials were accidentally delivered here, and it was deemed too difficult to move them. But even here construction was difficult. A staircase had to be carved into solid rock to move the pieces into places. The lighthouse is still in active use today.

When you do see a whale, there is little doubt about what it is. The water they spout is especially easy to see if the ocean is calm, and it is usually followed by the arching back of the whale itself. Once a whale surfaces, it is common to see it or others surface nearby again and again. It is worth the hours of staring at the sea when a graceful animal finally allows itself to be seen.

The changing sands are another fascinating feature of the Oregon Coast. At Alsea Bay, the sand spit grows to the south as much as ten feet per year. Farther south, forty-two miles of truly impressive sand dunes shift in the winds at the Oregon Dunes National Recreation Area. More than seven hundred feet high in places, these are the largest oceanside dunes in the world. They move north in winter and south in summer, covering plants and roads along the way.

To see the top of a tree poking out from a sand dune is to see evidence of an overwhelming power that is moving at a pace almost too slow to comprehend. Grain by grain, the prevailing winds move the sand around and behind any object that protrudes. Over time, a shrine-like hollow may surround the object, or an unlikely shelf tower above it.

Finally, a single grain of sand proves too much for the fragile structure, and a minuscule avalanche buries the object, providing a clean slate waiting to be textured again, this time starting at a slightly higher elevation than before.

▷ Sunset lingers in the sky at Devil's Elbow State Park, as one more wave reaches shore—and the endless rhythm continues. Just south of here is Sea Lion Caves, the largest natural sea caves in North America. The floor of the main chamber measures two acres. The only known mainland breeding site for the species, the caves also provide winter haven for a herd of Steller sea lions.

◁ Highway 101 follows the coastline for most of its 344 miles in
Oregon. Since 1940, it has been straightened enough to lose fifty miles.
△ Oregonians warmly welcomed Keiko, star of the movie, "Free Willy,"
to the Oregon Coast Aquarium in Newport.

△ Snare traps are used with fishing poles to take crab from the surf at
Siletz Bay, near Taft. ▷ Weathered clapboard buildings are typical
along the Oregon Coast, making a good backdrop for local bounty.

Fishing is a popular recreation on the coast, and the broad bays and estuaries teem with possibilities—from bottom fish like perch and ling cod, to shellfish such as clams, mussels, and crab. Most can be reeled in year-round, but the legendary Northwest salmon can be harvested only from May to September. Native Americans still have treaty fishing rights in some areas; salmon sustained their ancestors and played an important role in their culture. Commercial fleets now bring in albacore tuna, rockfish, sole, whiting, clams, mussels, baby shrimp, and at least ten million pounds of crab per season.

◁ Lazy, sunny days provide a brief respite from the fog and rain for those lucky enough to find the time to fish for the "big one." △ Waves explode against the cliffs at Rocky Creek Wayside.

△ Nye Beach was one of the earliest tourist destinations on the Oregon Coast. Summer people commuted by train from Corvallis and Portland.
▷ Weathered sandstones and basalt dominate Seal Rock State Park. Seals and sea lions can be seen here year-round.

The rugged profile of the Oregon Coast is the product of a volcanic past, an active geology, and millenniums of erosion; the forces of nature continue to sculpt its dramatic headlands and plentiful sea stacks. As powerful waves pound at the sea-cliffs, the softer rock is worn away, only to be washed in again as sand for the beaches. Tougher areas of volcanic basalt resist longer, jutting out as capes and headlands. The sea then searches out weak spots, or faults, in the volcanic rock, and breaks in to carve caves, blow holes, and spouting horns. Over time, arches ollapse, leaving sea stacks standing lone and imposing offshore.

Oregon's twenty-two estuaries are really drowned river valleys, created by rising seas after the last ice age. This meeting place of fresh and salt water is a complex environment that nourishes hundreds of species—bottom fish, shellfish, spawning ocean fish, salmon gaining strength to swim upstream, seals, and a multitude of birds, including eagles and great blue heron.

◁ Fresh water from Big Creek reaches the end of the line as it meets the Pacific Ocean. △ The Siuslaw River, which means "Faraway Waters," provided transportation to the early settlers in small towns such as Mapleton, situated upriver from Florence.

△ The Oregon Dunes National Recreation Area reaches from north of Florence south to Coos Bay. ▷ Cummins Creek flows through Neptune State Park at journey's end from Cummins Creek Wilderness. ▷▷ Headlands catch the rising mists south of Devil's Elbow State Park.

Wilderness beauty is protected and ejoyed in seventeen state parks along the Oregon Coast—a total of twenty-eight thousand acres. All the parks but one contain campgrounds with drive-in access, hot and cold water, showers, and motor home facilities. At Oswald West, campers hike in, trundling gear in wheelbarrows, in excange for extra peace and quiet. State park campgrounds are so popular that securing a weekend tent site requires advance reservations. Other park amenities include public docks, plentiful picnic sites, and miles of well-marked walking and hiking trails. Wildlife, unique flora, spectacular views, and healing solitude are usually just minutes away from the parking lot.

◁ The Umpqua River lighthouse boasts the only red lens on the U.S. West Coast. It sits to the south of the Umpqua River, the largest river between the Columbia and San Francisco. △ At Devils Elbow State Park, arches under Highway 101 throw graceful shadows on the beach.

△ The beaches of Oregon provide fertile grounds for numerous species of wildlife, including seabirds. ▷ Coos Head protects the marina at Charleston Harbor on the south slough of Coos Bay. The slough was the nation's first estuarine sanctuary.

THE SOUTH COAST

Native Americans first arrived in Oregon about ten thousand years ago. Their settlements on the coast spread from the north. Mild winters, tempered by marine air, made snow and ice infrequent, especially the farther south they traveled. The hunting and harvesting seasons were long. When the cold weather did arrive, preparation of preserved food took up the days, along with games and crafting goods for use and trade.

Native American art and artifacts found along the Oregon Coast show a highly developed aesthetic quality, even in everyday items. Many women were skilled basket makers, and different designs were popular in different regions. Cedar root and branch baskets, prized for their utility, were made beautiful by the addition of porcupine quills and vegetable stains. Wooden and shell beads were crafted, and certain types, especially those traded with other tribes, demonstrated the wealth of the owner. Native Americans wore beautifully sewn clothing of animal skins, while plant materials such as cedar bark, grasses, and rushes were made into petticoats and skirts. Shells and rocks provided unique adornment. Arrowheads and spear points, useful tools that are beautiful to look at, were made from many glass-like rocks, including obsidian traded from Central Oregon.

Today, Native Americans are respected for their relationship with the environment and the care they took in harvesting native species. They gave nature time to replenish herself, leaving an encampment before the surrounding land became too degraded to

◁ Clear days like this one at Shore Acres State Park can occur in both winter and summer, but fog, wind, and rain are more common. Rain averages sixty inches per year on the central coast, eighty inches on the south coast, and up to one hundred inches on the north coast. The Coast Range, which catches much of the rain moving inland, receives up to two hundred inches per year.

be easily restored. Their way of life can serve as a lesson and a challenge to those of us who use and enjoy the Oregon Coast today.

Coos Bay, the Oregon Coast's largest metropolitan area, is named for the Coos Tribe. The city grew up around the largest ocean-side port between Puget Sound and San Francisco. The bay was carved out by the rush of melting ice following the last Ice Age ten thousand years ago. Coos Bay, long a timber center, has suffered from the decline in that industry as well as in commercial fishing. For a time, the working town seemed destined to grayness and obscurity. Today, the people of the region are designing a bright new future focusing on the great bay as a trading center. Ships from around the world stop here for repairs. New industries, from cranberry cultivation to module fabrication, are being developed. Coos Bay has become a prime destination for retirees looking for a place on the Oregon Coast.

From Bandon southward, spectacular large rocks and sea stacks make the Southern Oregon Coast one of the wildest and most scenic places in the world. Many beaches are guarded by outcroppings of rock that have withstood the torturous pressures of the ocean for thousands of years. These naturally sculpted formations have acquired descriptive names such as Tower Rock, Castle Rock, West Conical Rock and Arch Rock. Stop at the Bandon Ocean State Wayside and stare at Face Rock for a few moments, and suddenly the tilted face appears like magic.

▷ Streams and rivers like the Millacoma drain into Coos Bay, formed by the massive flow of melting ice at the end of the last ice age ten thousand years ago. Golden and Silver Falls State Park is home to two dramatic falls and a stand of old-growth forest, including Douglas fir, myrtlewood, alder, and big leaf maple. This rushing water is in Glenn Creek, just below Golden Falls.

In addition to dozens of state waysides, eighty of Oregon's two hundred state parks are located on the coast. Oregon's beaches had been set aside by Governor Oswald West in 1915 for "public highway." As horse and carriage traffic gave way to automobiles and roads were developed, the State Park Commission, established in 1929, was quick to make parks of many of the beaches. They are a popular state asset. Camping, fishing, picnicking, beachcombing and birdwatching opportunities abound. Many parks also include interesting interpretive signs and displays explaining local history and natural resources. You can learn about Native American settlements, the pioneer experience, rare plants, birds and wildlife. Some coastal parks feature beautiful lighthouses, today as much beacons to visitors as warnings to ships. Nine lighthouses, built between 1857 and 1934, grace Oregon's rugged coastline.

◁ Shore Acres State Park incompasses the formal gardens of the Simpson Estate, built in 1906. The Simpsons cultivated two hundred acres with plants brought from around the world on his ships. Today, the conservatory houses rare plants. The sunken Oriental garden remains, as do lawns and beds that are now maintained by park personnel and a non-profit support organization.

Scouting for driftwood is a favorite recreational hobby. A walk along almost any of Oregon's beaches will yield fanciful creations of the waves, especially after a winter storm. Decorated driftwood is a staple at church bazaars and in many small shops. Driftwood collecting can be serious fun; many Oregon yards, on the coast as well as inland, feature both large and small pieces that take their owners back to a special walk on the beach. We've heard that the largest driftwood collection in the world is located in Bandon.

A beachcombing expedition may also yield treasures that have broken away from boats at sea. The glass floats popular with Japanese fleets, especially in past decades, were always something to look for while walking on the beach. Unfortunately, trash also washes ashore, becoming both a hazard to wildlife as well as unsightly. Concerned Oregonians responded to this problem by organizing the world's first volunteer beach cleanup in 1984. This event now draws between four and six thousand caring beachgoers twice a year. The idea has also spread to more than thirty other states and forty foreign countries.

Southern Oregon juts so far out into the Pacific Ocean that no city in the continental United States is farther west than Port Orford. A trail onto Cape Blanco, five miles to the north, brings you to the westernmost point and spectacular panoramic views. This is the site of the Cape Blanco Lighthouse, the oldest working lighthouse on the Oregon Coast. Built in 1870, it guides ships around reefs made more dangerous by winter winds that often gust to one hundred miles per hour or more.

Port Orford is situated on a unique natural ocean harbor, Oregon's only harbor that is not a river outlet and has no bar to cross. Port Orford also has the West Coast's only crane docking system, hoisting commercial boats out of the water at day's end and returning them each morning for another day of fishing.

Brookings, the Oregon Coast's southernmost city, is well known for its temperate climate. Winter temperatures average 40 to 50 degrees. January readings in the 70s are not uncommon. The area is ideally suited

▷ Tree fungus prefers old-growth forest as habitat but can sometimes be found on younger trees as well. Temperate rain levels have covered much of Oregon's coastal lands, and logging has been a primary support of coastal communities. Old-growth or secondary-growth forests, encompassing a rich variety of flora and fauna, can be found on many of the headlands of the coast.

for the growth of Easter lilies; 90% of the country's supply is grown here and in northern California.

More people move to Oregon's coast each year; more visitors tour its towns and beaches. Our challenge is to recognize the fragility that is sometimes hidden by the power of the waves and storms. One person leaving a designated pathway to a beach may not make much of an impact. But if hordes of people follow, they soon extinguish the life from the club moss that grew there. Removing one starfish from a tidal pool may not seem to make a difference. But what purpose does it serve when that starfish is soon dead? And what loss is suffered when all of the starfish are gone?

Oregonians' pride of place has long contributed to the state's sense of worth and created a commitment to conservation and stewardship. Perhaps nowhere in Oregon are the benefits more apparent than on the magnificent Oregon Coast. Here every beach, from the low tide mark to where regular vegetation grows, is public property. No fences bar us from walking along sandy beaches; no developments spill down to the water's edge; no private property signs keep us from accessing the shore.

Tom McCall, Oregon's champion and its governor from 1967 to 1974, helped establish land use laws that make the state's development unique by checking urban sprawl and reserving prime farm and forest lands exclusively for those purposes. He introduced the nation's first bottle pollution control, and open space

◁ The Cape Arago lighthouse sits on a small island called Gregory Point at Coos Bay's entrance. This is the third lighthouse built here; the first two were lost to the encroachment of the sea on the island's sandstone cliffs. It is believed that Sir Francis Drake visited the area in 1579. James Cook dubbed it Cape Gregory in 1778, but the name was changed to Cape Arago in 1850.

bills and founded SOLV, Stop Oregon Litter and Vandalism. But many people believe his greatest legacy was ensuring that Oregon's beaches would forever be held in the public trust.

His official portrait in the state capitol in Salem shows McCall at the water's edge, measuring to determine how much of the shore should be declared public beach. This was done by erecting a sixteen-foot pole at the low tide mark, with a string of the same length attached at its top. The string was then walked inland, across the beach, to where it met the rising land. This exercise confirmed the scientific theory that below this point was generally sand and dunes, so the measurement was used to define Oregon's public beaches.

Whether you are a visitor or an Oregonian heading for your favorite spot on the beach, Oregon's magnificent coast produces images that shine in your memory like the sun shimmering off gentle waves on a warm August day. Whatever our interests—history, geology, wildlife, botany, sightseeing, or shopping—she has something to offer each of us.

When we take the magnificent Oregon Coast on her own terms, she exhilarates us and is generous with her many splendid moods. In return, we need only to tread carefully and leave as little impact as possible. To leave her with no impact from our presence is the responsibility we carry with us, and the legacy we leave to those who will come after us.

▷ A rusty boat at Bandon reflects the slow-down of the fishing industry, being replaced today by dairy farming and other agricultural endeavors. Cranberries, first brought to Coos County from a natural bog in Cape Cod by Charles Dexter McFarlin, have been cultivated in this region since 1885. Cranberry bogs, their vines filling marshy areas, can be seen from Highway 101.

◁ The Coquille River lighthouse at Bandon was built in 1896 and decommissioned after forty-three years of service. △ At Bandon State Park, the sun turns the waves to pewter.

△ Lord George Bennett of Ireland brought gorse to the Bandon area
in the 1890s to remind him of home. The citizens of Bandon have
fought its spread, but it continues to overtake native vegetation today.
▷ Groves of kelp shelter fish and marine mammals.

Thick forests of laminara, large kelp, form in the intertidal zones. Nemocystis, bull or ribbon kelp, grows more than thirty meters tall. Washed ashore, it looks like a bull whip. The hollow ball or holdfast, with its small, entangled root system, is refuge for small animals. Sea otters play in the kelp and wrap strands around their bodies when they sleep. They also protect the kelp beds by consuming sea urchins.

Some fifteen to twenty thousand gray whales pass these coasts twice a year, journeying from arctic to sub-tropic waters. Their six-thousand-mile migration is the longest of any mammal. Pregnant females pass the Oregon Coast in December and January, heading south. Northward migration peaks here about mid-March, and cows with calves pass by from May through early June. Recently, about two hundred gray whales have ended their migration to spend summer and fall off the Oregon Coast. Whales are often seen from coastal promontories; calm, overcast mornings are best for watching.

◁ Whalehead Cove is a day-use area in Sam Boardman State Park,
named for Oregon state parks' first superintendent. △ Arch Rock is one
of hundreds of seastacks along the southern Oregon Coast. ▷ ▷ Skunk
cabbage bears the largest leaves of any plant in the northwestern U.S.

83

△ Steeply rising hills and headlands give bird's-eye views of beaches below. ▷ Found objects, especially fishing floats, combined with wood that has been weathered by the elements, decorate many coastal yards.

Serious beach-combers enjoy coastal winters, when giant waves hurl all manner of drift-wood and trea-sures high on the shore. Winter brings strong southwest winds, heavy rains, and the year's highest tides. In sum-mer, the North Pacific High dominates. Winds circle it clockwise, result-ing in steady north winds and often fog. Coastal tem-peratures are generally milder than inland.

◁ Port Orford is the only remaining place on the West Coast where boats are docked by crane and wagon. △ At Gold Beach, the Weddweburn Bridge crosses the rugged Rogue River, well known for its white-water rafting and its jet boating.

△ The Rogue River brought precious metals from inland, giving Gold Beach its name. ▷ Seastacks and sand dunes rise before Cape Sebastian, which ascends 715 feet. ▷▷ Fog, rain, and wind are common on the Oregon Coast. Oregonians appreciate those rare clear days.

Almost half of the 362-mile-long Oregon Coast is bordered by dunes, more than in either Washington or California. This sandy shore is in constant flux. Dunes shift north in winter and south in summer with the prevailing winds. In winter, beaches shrink as sand washes out to sea. It piles up in bars, then summer's gentler waves wash it in again.